Ciffer gave me this
book — summer 1990.
Took ~~boys~~ to second hand
book store in the
New Carrollton Library!

NANCY LOPEZ
GOLFING PIONEER

Library of Congress Cataloging in Publication Data

Hahn, James.
  Nancy Lopez: golfing pioneer.

  (The Champions and challengers 2)
  SUMMARY: A biography of the young woman from New
Mexico who has fought sexual and ethnic discrimination
to become a successful professional golfer.
  1. Lopez, Nancy, 1957-   —Juvenile literature. 2.
Golfers—United States—Biography—Juvenile literature.
[1. Lopez, Nancy, 1957-   2. Golfers]
I. Hahn, Lynn, joint author. II. Title. III. Series.
GV964.L67H33   796.352'092'4 [B] [92]   78-13162
ISBN 0-88436-480-1

Published 1979. Produced by EMC Corporation
180 East Sixth Street, Saint Paul, Minnesota 55101
Printed in the United States of America
0 9 8 7 6 5 4 3 2 1

NANCY LOPEZ
GOLFING PIONEER

BY JAMES & LYNN HAHN

EMC CORPORATION ST. PAUL, MINNESOTA

PHOTO CREDITS

All photography by Jeffrey Blackman.
Cover photography by Jeffrey Blackman.

On Sunday afternoon, March 12, 1978, many people were still recovering from one of the worst winters in history. But on the Rancho Park Golf Course in Los Angeles, California, the sun was shining and it was 66°.

Thousands of fans were following the women professional golfers playing in the $100,000 Sunstar tournament. Many fans were Mexican-Americans, proud to be watching Nancy Lopez, the first Mexican-American woman to be successful on the Ladies Professional Golfer's Association (LPGA) tour.

Nancy was only 21 years old then. She hadn't been a golf pro for a year yet. Still a rookie, she played like a veteran. Already, she had impressed millions of golf fans with long, powerful drives, accurate putting, determination, courage, and friendliness. Whether she's winning or losing, feeling good or hurting, a warm, wide, genuine smile brightens her face.

"That's what I do when I get excited," Nancy says, "I smile."

On that afternoon at Rancho Park, Nancy was smiling, even though after seven holes she was five strokes behind the leaders. With the same determination she had shown many times before in her life, Nancy refused to give up. Thousands of fans cheered and applauded as she made par after par on the tough Rancho Park Golf Course.

By the 16th hole, this determined young woman from Roswell, New Mexico had made up the five strokes. She was tied for the lead with veteran golfers Debbie Austin and Debbie Massey!

Nancy says her powerful swing comes from practicing.

On the 17th green, Nancy had an 18-foot putt for a birdie. If she could sink it, she would be the leader.

Nancy stroked her putt slowly and smoothly. The ball rolled towards the hole. Plunk! It dropped in for a birdie! Nancy's fans cheered!

The 18th hole is a 366-yard long par four. Nancy's drive was fine. But she made a mistake on her second shot. She hit it short of the green. Debbie Austin almost sank her second shot. But her ball rolled eight feet past the hole.

Then, Nancy made another mistake. She hit her chip shot too hard. It rolled seven feet past the cup.

Debbie Austin putted. Her ball rolled into the cup for a birdie!

When Nancy has to sink a putt under pressure, she takes her time.

Nancy had to sink her seven-foot putt to win the tournament. She stroked her putt. The ball rolled slowly. Finally, it dropped into the cup!

Nancy Lopez won the tournament and $15,000. It was her second Ladies Professional Golfer's Association victory in a row! She won her first at Bent Tree, in Sarasota, Florida on February 26, 1978.

Wiping tears from her cheeks and speaking softly, Nancy told reporters after her victory, "I owe everything in golf to my mother and father. My father has always been my teacher. He taught me to be competitive." After wiping away more tears, Nancy smiled and continued, "You'll have to pardon me. I feel kind of spacey and emotional about what happened today. I just can't believe this. I never dreamed I could be this successful this quickly. I'm so happy that my father was here. When I won at Bent Tree I felt as though it was for my mother, and this one was for my father. They are the main reasons I play golf."

Though Nancy loves to smile, she's all business about her golf game.

Luck or magic didn't help Nancy win that $15,000 in Los Angeles. Her golf skills won the tournament. It took years of practice, hard work, discipline, sacrifices, disappointments, and discouragements to develop those skills. Before she won her first professional golf tournament, Nancy had to solve money problems. She had to overcome racial and sexual discrimination.

Nancy's climb to the top of the women's golfing world began when she was born on January 26, 1957. Domingo and Marina Lopez were her proud parents.

Domingo, a small, but sturdy man, worked in the corn and cotton fields around Roswell, New Mexico as a tenant farmer. He saved his money until he had enough to open a small auto repair shop. It was so small, it only had room for two cars. But Domingo worked hard and after a few years he expanded his shop so he could work on 12 cars at the same time.

On Sunday afternoons, Domingo played golf on Roswell's public golf course. Marina played too, because her doctor told her she needed exercise. Little Nancy tagged along because there was no one home to take care of her. Domingo played golf skillfully. Usually, he shot only a few strokes over par.

In 1964, when Nancy was just seven, she told her parents she wanted to play golf too. "I kept pestering my father to let me hit a golf ball," she says.

Finally, Domingo gave Nancy a golf ball, a tee, and her mother's 4-wood. He said, "Hit the ball and keep up with us."

In the beginning, Nancy struggled just to swing the heavy clubs. Today she doesn't even seem to struggle with the real problem shots.

"I kept hitting and hitting and hitting," Nancy says, "struggling to stay ahead of the next group of grown-ups." But little Nancy didn't give up. She says she was determined to hit that little white ball as well as her father hit it.

"Pretty soon," Nancy says, "Daddy saw my ball rolling past his feet." Then, she started hitting the ball over his head.

"I couldn't believe my little daughter could hit the ball so far," Domingo says. "I got excited and told Marina, 'Maybe Nancy can really play!'"

"I didn't know what I was doing then," Nancy confessed. "I was just swinging at the ball and having a good time. But I liked golf from the beginning."

Marina realized how much her daughter enjoyed golf. But she told Domingo it cost too much money to have three golfers in the family. Marina finally gave up golf so her husband and daughter could play together. She gave Nancy her golf clubs.

Nancy thanked her mother and started practicing and playing golf almost every day. "I practiced as long as possible," she says.

Nancy's golf game improved so quickly that in 1966, when she was only nine years old, she played in her first golf tournament—a Pee Wee tournament for girls 12 years old and younger.

The tournament was held 110 miles from Roswell in Alamogordo, New Mexico. Nancy and the other girls played nine holes a day for three days. After all the scores were added, the officials announced that Nancy Lopez had won.

When Nancy was 10, she played in the 1967 Roswell Ladies' Golf Tournament. After golfer Jo Boswell won, Nancy says she cried because she wanted to win. "I want to be as good a golfer as Mrs. Boswell," Nancy told her father.

Hugging his daughter, Domingo replied, "Nancy, be as good as Mrs. Boswell, and a little bit better."

Nancy practiced for several hours every day to improve. "I gave up my free time to practice," she says.

But Nancy didn't practice all the time. Once, after she had her beautiful, black, waist-length hair cut into a pixie-style, she cried for three days.

To crack long drives, Nancy needs powerful arms.

Nancy recovered and went back to practicing. But she felt disappointment again when she was 11. Jo Boswell beat her by three strokes in the 1968 Roswell Ladies' Golf tournament.

Instead of giving up, Nancy practiced more and improved. The 11-year-old improved so much she decided to play in New Mexico's Women's Amateur tournament.

Nancy surprised many golfers, fans and reporters when she qualified for the championship by shooting an 84! Then she won two matches. But she lost to the defending champion on the 18th hole. Again she cried and cried.

Domingo, wiping the tears off Nancy's cheeks, advised, "If you want to play good, you have to get beat. That's how you learn."

That loss, Nancy says, taught her she had to practice still more. Determined to be a winner, Nancy practiced and practiced. Then, she practiced some more.

While she practiced, Nancy says she thought about what her father had told her about golf. "Swing slowly. Move the club away from the ball slowly. Come up slowly and high. Then hit the ball in the sweet spot."

After many, many hours of practice, Nancy started cracking long drives down the middle of the fairway.

When Domingo saw Nancy's improvements, he says he and Marina decided to sacrifice so Nancy could play more golf. Domingo worked overtime in his auto repair shop and Marina shopped for bargains. She didn't buy expensive clothes or foods.

Nancy's determination, persistence, and hard work began to pay off in 1969. When she was 12, she finally beat veteran golfer Jo Boswell in the Roswell Ladies' Golf Tournament!

That same year, Nancy accomplished an even greater golfing feat! She won New Mexico's Women's Amateur Championship! The little 12-year-old girl defeated women 10, 20, and 30 years older than herself!

Although Nancy had achieved great success, it was hard for her to become even more successful. This young golfing pioneer felt a lot of pressure. Before some tournaments, Nancy says she was so nervous she chewed her fingernails down to the quick. She vomited so many times before important matches, she says she made a habit of dressing in the bathroom.

But the more Nancy played the less she chewed her nails and vomited. Gradually, she gained confidence and poise. Still, Nancy says she sometimes felt her legs jiggling nervously.

In 1970, when she was 13, Nancy won the New Mexico Women's Amateur again. She won it for the third time when she was 14! Nancy had become a successful amateur golfer, but she had to conquer an ugly problem—racial prejudice.

Nancy grew up playing on a flat public course without any sandtraps. She handles them like a pro today.

Many country clubs let outstanding young amateurs play on their golf courses for free. Nancy was the most outstanding young amateur in Roswell. But a country club there didn't give Nancy any free rounds of golf because she was a Mexican-American.

The country club's officials said Nancy could play golf on their course if her father bought a membership. They knew Domingo could never afford their expensive fees.

After Nancy achieved professional golfing success in 1978 she said, "Because I was a Mexican, there were a lot of Anglos in Roswell who weren't ready to accept the kind of golf I was playing. Now a lot of them like to say they are my friends. But I don't feel I owe them my friendship because they didn't give me theirs when I was young. My parents gave me all the chances I ever needed."

Discrimination made Nancy work harder. She spent hour after hour on Roswell's public golf course, chipping, putting, and driving hundreds of golf balls. Nancy Lopez was determined to rise above racial prejudice.

In August 1972, this 15-year-old Mexican-American received national acclaim when she won her first national golfing title—the United States Golf Association's (USGA) Girls' Junior Championship.

The victory didn't come easy, though. Nancy had to work hard for it. With two holes left in match play, she was losing, one hole down. On the 17th green, Nancy sank a 25-foot putt to tie the match! On the 18th, she had to make one of the hardest shots in golf, a six-foot downhill putt. Nancy stroked the ball. It rolled, curved, and finally slid into the cup!

After that victory, Nancy Lopez was ranked the number one girl golfer in the country. She went on to win another major tournament—the Western Junior Girls.

Nancy's golf skills amazed many of her competitors and their parents. They wondered why Nancy was so skillful. She never had expensive lessons from a golf professional. She didn't play on a lush country club course. To many, because of their prejudice, she was just a Mexican-American who played on a flat public course in New Mexico. They didn't know that Nancy worked harder and was more dedicated and determined to win than most youngsters.

Nancy made many sacrifices for golf.

As a teenager, Nancy began dedicating her life to golf. She sacrificed many activities for golf. She says she didn't go swimming because the water softened her golf calluses and the strokes made her use muscles that hurt her golfing muscles. She tried tennis, but sprained her ankle and got scared that it would hurt her golf.

In high school, Nancy had to face another big problem—sexism. Although she was a better golfer than most of the boys, she was not allowed to play on the Goddard High School golf team because she was a girl.

This golfing pioneer didn't let that stop her. Nancy, with a lawyer, went to the Board of Education and argued that the school should let the best *golfers* play on the team, not just the best boys. After listening to Nancy, the Board agreed to let her play.

But playing on the golf team wasn't easy either. At one match in March, Nancy says her hands were freezing before she even teed off. Nancy played anyway. It started to rain on the ninth hole. Nancy says she felt like quitting then, but was determined to keep on playing.

On the 14th, when it started hailing, Nancy walked off the course. The coach told her to go back out. Nancy says she told herself, "If I quit, he might not let me back on the team."

Nancy went out and finished the back nine, shooting a 41. Then she went to the washroom to wash the mud off her slacks. When she finished, the coach said the match was tied, there was going to be a play-off, and she had to go back out and play. "We won on the first hole." Nancy says, "Thank goodness!"

That season, Nancy and the Goddard High Rockets won the state championship, defeating Albuquerque High by four strokes. Shooting a 77 and an 82, Nancy placed fifth in individual scoring.

Nancy helped Goddard High win another state championship. When she was a senior, Nancy was the best golfer on the team. She finished fourth in the state championship that year.

Nancy has given new life to professional golf. But in the beginning, she faced discrimination because she was female.

During the summer, Nancy played in national tournaments. Traveling to these tournaments cost a lot of money. Domingo and Marina worked hard, but couldn't afford all Nancy's golf expenses. Impressed with Nancy's determination and friendly personality, the Roswell Seniors and Retirees gave a banquet for her in 1973. Then the Chamber of Commerce donated $500 for her expenses at the Western Golf Association's Junior tournament, held in Wisconsin that year. Nancy won that tournament.

Nancy's parents had lots of financial worries. Nancy really appreciates their sacrifices.

Nancy's father helped her with golfing tips. Today she gets help from her caddie, Roscoe.

Nancy had enough money left to travel to the Women's Western Amateur, where she reached the semi-finals. The Lindells, a generous family from Winfield, Iowa, let Nancy stay in their home during the Western. After the tournament, they drove her home to New Mexico. Nancy had $100 left, so she returned it to the Chamber of Commerce.

Nancy understood the money pressures her mother and father were under. "I felt guilty because I knew I could get a pretty good job," she says. "I could type 65 words per minute. I was even willing to learn bookkeeping from my mother, who did it for my dad's business."

But Domingo didn't want his daughter to work. He says it would have tired her and taken too much time away from golf.

Being a hard-working golfer had its benefits too. Domingo says he told Marina not to let Nancy do the dishes because the hot, soapy water would hurt her hands.

During the summer of 1974, Domingo and Marina spent about $3,000 on Nancy's golf. They said they were happy to do it. But Domingo said, "Maybe Nancy will see she can make a lot of money playing golf and then she'll let me and Momma rest."

Nancy appreciated her parents' hard work and practiced many hours so she wouldn't waste their money.

"Golf is my life," Nancy said when she was 17. But playing in amateur tournaments throughout the country isn't as easy as some people think. Sometimes Nancy got homesick. "I think about my family and friends when I'm away from home," she admitted. But she added, "I put my mind on golf when I'm playing."

In the summer of 1975, 18-year-old Nancy surprised golfers, fans, reporters, and millions of TV viewers. She finished second in the most important golf tournament in the world for women—the United States Open!

On a rugged, wind-swept golf course near Atlantic City, New Jersey, Nancy shot rounds of 73, 74, 77, and 75. Sandra Palmer won, but Nancy finished ahead of many veteran pros.

At the post-tournament press conference, Nancy said she wasn't ready to become a professional golfer yet. "I just don't think being 18 and being on the tour mix very well. Once you turn pro, you have to believe that your entire life is to be directed toward golf. I'm just not ready to do that yet, although I love golf. Right now I just want to enjoy being young, and playing golf as part of my life, but not all of it. I want to get involved in other things. I think these years coming up are important in a young person's life and I want to get all I can out of them."

Nancy squeezed all she could out of her late teens. She went to parties, danced and talked. She and her friends spent many happy hours cruising down Main Street in Roswell and munching on burgers and fries.

Nancy and Roscoe talk over a disappointing moment.

After doing so well in the U.S. Open, Nancy experienced some bitter disappointments later that year. She lost in the semi-finals at the Western Amateur, lost in the second round of the U.S. Amateur, and blew a five hole lead in the Trans-National tournament. But she didn't give up. Instead she practiced more.

Planning with Roscoe, Nancy realizes that golfers have to think things out.

In the fall of 1975, Nancy entered the University of Tulsa. Her golf skills earned her a $10,000 Colgate Golf Scholarship. She was happy because her father and mother didn't have to pay so many golf bills. "It's easier on them now," she said at the time.

At Tulsa, Nancy studied engineering. She also worked to improve her golf skills with Coach Dale McNamara. It wasn't all work and no play, though. Some evenings, Nancy and her teammates gathered in the coach's home for soft drink parties and talk sessions.

Nancy's unselfish personality earned the respect of her college coach. It earns her hundreds of fans today.

During the 1976 college golf season, Nancy helped Tulsa win many matches. Coach McNamara says Nancy was a very unselfish team player whose influence on the other girls was healthy. That year Nancy became the best woman college golfer in the country when she won the Association for Intercollegiate Athletics for Women (AIAW) tournament.

That summer Nancy won the Western Women's Amateur and the Trans-National Amateur. Then she helped the United States win the World Amateur Women's Team Championship in Portugal.

"Getting to play in the World Team was really neat," Nancy says. "I wanted to play well, representing my country. Meeting those women from all over the world was great. I especially liked to watch what they wore. The women from Portugal, for instance, they were different in their long, tight shorts and knee-high socks."

A successful international golfer, Nancy still had to face disappointments. After failing to qualify for the final 36 holes in the 1976 U.S. Open, Nancy said, "That hurt, especially when I finished second in 1975."

In June 1977, after her sophomore year at Tulsa, 20-year-old Nancy decided to become a professional golfer. "It was time to start earning money," she says. "I didn't want my parents to sacrifice and work any more."

Nancy said once she started making some money, she wanted to buy her parents a house.

The 1977 U.S. Open was the first tournament Nancy played in as a pro. She surprised many veterans when she finished two strokes behind the winner, Hollis Stacy! Nancy Lopez's first paycheck was $7,040!

Nancy went from paper name tags to very expensive ones when she decided to turn pro.

Before any woman can play on the women's pro tour, she must qualify in the LPGA qualifying tournament. Nancy played under a lot of pressure at the tournament because the competition was so intense. Forty-eight other women wanted to make their living by joining the pro tour too.

Nancy withstood the pressure and qualified. After qualifying, Nancy cried. She told reporters her parents had worked so hard, and now she was finally a professional golfer. Wiping away tears, Nancy said she would practice extra hard so her mother and father would be proud of her.

The Colgate-European Women's Open In Berkshire, England was Nancy's second tournament as a pro. She got so homesick she had to call her parents in Roswell. After the call, Nancy felt better. Playing in the wind and rain, she shot 72, 71, 73, and 71 to finish second, behind Judy Rankin. Nancy's second paycheck was $9,750!

The Long Island Classic in New York was Nancy's third tournament as a pro. The amazing rookie finished second for the third time in a row! Her third paycheck was $8,375!

Nancy's finish was courageous, because she had torn a ligament in her right hand during the European Open. She had been playing with pain. Eventually, Nancy missed three tournaments and couldn't play golf for a month because her hand hurt so much.

Nancy believes that making the putts makes money.

Nancy has lots of fire, courage, and determination.

Her mother's death hurt. It also gave her more determination than ever
to win.

Nancy says she used her time off to find out why she wasn't winning tournaments. "Being second three times in a row made me put pressure on myself. I expected to do better every tournament. When I did worse, I felt the whole world coming down on top of me," she says.

Nancy rejoined the tour, but in the fall of 1977 she quit playing again because she had to overcome a tragedy. Marina, Nancy's hard-working mother, who had sacrificed so much so her daughter could play golf, died September 29th from an infection after an appendectomy.

After her mother's death, Nancy says she felt strange. "I've seen death on television but it was hard for me to understand my own mother's death."

Nancy says whenever she played golf, she had played for her mother and father. After her mother died, Nancy says there was something missing. "I lost my spark. It was the worst thing that ever happened to me."

But gradually, Nancy says, she regained her spark. She promised to play the best golf she could for her mother.

That spark burst into a bright flame in late January, 1978, when Nancy defeated the tournament favorite, Judy Rankin, in the first round of the Colgate Triple Crown match play championship.

As Nancy walked away from the green, she started crying. "I was thinking of my mother," she says. During the match, Nancy says she felt like her mother was with her. It was a happy feeling. Though she did not go on to win the tournament, Nancy says she had regained her competitive spirit.

That bright flame exploded into a roaring fire in February and March! On February 26, 1978, at the Bent Tree Classic in Sarasota, Florida, Nancy won her first pro tournament! It was worth $15,000. Wiping tears out of her eyes, Nancy dedicated the victory to the memory of her mother.

After winning her second tournament, the Sunstar Classic, in Los Angeles, Nancy traveled to San Diego to play in the Kathryn Crosby Classic. In a thrilling nationally-televised tournament, Nancy lost to Sally Little in a sudden death play-off. But she still earned $14,650.

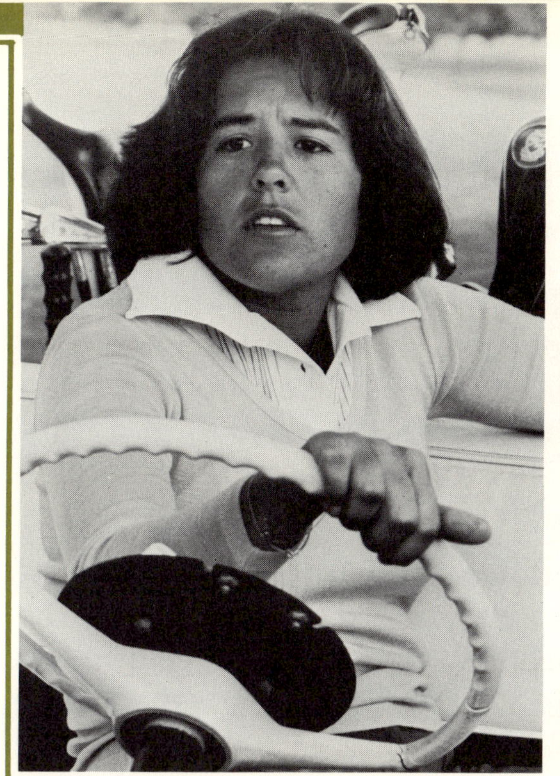

Older players have to take Nancy seriously. She has really challenged them.

In just 12 weeks the Mexican-American from Roswell had zoomed to the top of the LPGA money list! Nancy had earned $47,317 in just a few tournaments. Yet with all her successes came more problems that had to be solved.

During the next tournament, the Colgate-Dinah Shore Winners Circle, Nancy shot a 76, her worst round of 1978. She says she felt a lot of pressure. Magazine, newspaper, radio, and TV reporters all wanted to interview her. Crowds of people followed her around the golf course. Friends and relatives came to visit "famous" Nancy.

"People forgot that I'm human," was Nancy's reaction to all the pressure. "I don't know if it's an emotional breakdown or what, but I don't feel happy right now. My life is changing and I don't know if I want it to. So many things matter to me—how I look, how people feel about me, what my friends are doing—and now golf is so serious. The other day I told everybody, 'Look, this isn't a party. It's a golf tournament!' Then I felt terrible for being such a crab."

Nancy, reaching down deep to tap all her ability, personality, and maturity, overcame most of the pressure. She recovered enough to finish 12th in the tournament. Her $4,455 paycheck pushed her earnings up to $51,772.

By the middle of Nancy's rookie year, she had earned more money than any other rookie (male or female) in the history of professional golf. She also set a new record for the LPGA by winning five tournaments in a row. She had over $150,000 in prize money.

Although Nancy has achieved golfing success, she still must work hard to maintain her golf skills. She says she wants to keep on improving. So, she puts in many hours on the practice tee, trying to get rid of the wrist action in her swing and learning how to keep her hands firm.

Nancy is a skillful putter because she practices every day. "If you make those putts, you'll make money," she says. "I'm cheating myself when I go without practicing."

Nancy doesn't spend all her time practicing and golfing. But she has trouble finding ways to relax. "My work is playing golf," she says, "and I can't do anything to relax. I can't swim because it's bad for my hands and grip. I can't play tennis because it builds up my arms. All I can do is dance and lie around in the sun."

A cheerful, friendly person, Nancy does relax at tournament receptions where she meets such people as Arnold Palmer, Dinah Shore, Bob Hope, and President Ford.

It's hard for Nancy to find ways to relax.

Nancy was most outstanding rookie-male or female. Her fans call themselves, "Nancy's Navy."

Eating is one of Nancy's pleasures. But Nancy says she doesn't eat very much junk food or anything too fattening. She says you must be in good condition to play tournament golf.

Collecting classical music albums is one of the ways Nancy spends her free time. She says she also has fun listening to such modern musicians as Elton John and Barry Manilow. But "the Bee Gees are my favorites!"

Reading is another of Nancy's pastimes. She says her favorite authors are Ernest Hemingway and Robert Frost.

Nancy also enjoys shopping in the stores near where she's golfing. She hunts for bargains in shorts and tops (greens and yellows are her favorite colors), denim slacks, and nice evening dresses. "I want to look nice on the golf course," she says, "I don't want to become a sex symbol or anything like that, just look nice."

Driving her maroon-red Monte Carlo, with its AM/FM stereo radio and eight track tape deck, is another way Nancy relaxes. Her CB handle (citizens band radio nickname) is "Jive Cookie."

After a full day of golf and practice, Nancy says she enjoys resting and watching television in her motel room. She says sometimes she's a TV addict.

Wherever Nancy plays golf, young people ask her for advice. She tells them, "If you want to do something, you have to work hard and dedicate yourself to it."

When youngsters ask Nancy how they can become better golfers, she says "by working hard—practice."

Nancy says she recommends a career as a professional golfer because "it's a good sport. You can be an individual and you can receive a lot of self-satisfaction."

Because Nancy Lopez conquered racial and sexual discrimination, she is a golfing pioneer. Because she overcame money and personal problems, she is a sports heroine.

But, more importantly, no matter how many tournaments Nancy Lopez wins or doesn't win, her cheerful, friendly, out-going personality won't change. "I'll not get snobbish," she says, "I like to make friends too much for that."

GLOSSARY

back nine the second half of an eighteen hole course

birdie a hole scored in one stroke less than par

chip a short low shot that moves the ball in a high arc to the green and rolls it toward the hole

drive a ball hit toward the green from the tee

green a smooth, low-cut area of grass on which all putts are made, and which contains the hole into which the ball is played

hole the opening or cup into which the ball is played; also, the playing area from the tee to the hole, or cup

match a contest between players

par the number of strokes an expert golfer is expected to make on each hole based on distance

par four from 211 to 400 yards distance (women players), or 251 to 470 yards distance (men players)

putt any short stroke rolling the ball across the green

round a series of plays during which each of 18 holes is made in turn

semi-final the next to last round in a golf tournament

shoot to move or propel the ball toward the hole

sink a successful shot or stroke of the ball into the hole

stroke a forward move of the golf club toward the ball

sudden death play-off an extra period given to players to break a tie after the final round of regular play

swing the movement of the head of the golf club toward the ball

wood a golf club with a large wooden head used in driving the ball; numbered 1-5, with the higher numbered clubs lifting the ball in a higher arc toward the green